AF507350

The Gatekeeper Wears Acrylics

Copyright © 2023 Court Winterborne

Cover Art copyright © 2022 by Kylee Condelario

All rights reserved. No portion of this publication may be repro-duced,
stored in a retrieval system, or transmitted in any form
or by any other means, electronic, mechanical, photocopying, or
recording without prior permission of Court Winterborne unless
such copying is expressly permitted by federal copyright law.

Address inquiries in permissions to:
Echobird Press, echobirdpress.com
ISBN-13: 979-8-9863865-6-0 (Echobird Press)

For Q. For Jen.

For the past 20 years, you have filled the cracks of my heart
with gold.
Thank you for reminding me I am a tiger
when I feel like a mouse.

Acknowledgments

Thank you to Kat Crespin for being the first to publish my book _Wild Horses,_ giving a safe place for "Kalanchoe" "Snapdragons" "Closer to One" and "Aspens" to frolick. Your talent and compassion continues on in the legacy of authors you supported as the originator of Swimming with Elephants Publications.

Thank you to Kylee Condelario for the magnificent cover art! You brought my "Gatekeeper" to vivid life. As my tattoo artist in New Mexico, you always held space for the narrative of a piece, navigating emotional nuance with grace and understanding. You are unparalleled.

Thank you to Kat and Terra of EchoBird Press for supporting me through the process of bringing "The Gatekeeper Wears Acrylics" to life! It is a true privilege to work with you both.

And thank you to Matt. Thank God your love is neither subtle nor quiet. Being with you inspires and excites me for our future! I love you.

Table of Contents

Previously published in *Wild Horses

<u>*Tiger/Heart*</u>

The tiger in my chest is hungry

Trained to believe feeding a tiger is suicide –
I starved her
denied her

She is chained and crazed now

I ignored her like I was instructed to
Believed the authority of others over the quaking of my body
Received accolades for how diligently I hid her existence
from view

Desperately pretending she wasn't there
or
when her howls and growls became too much
convinced those within earshot
that she was just a house cat

Silenced her with a backhand through the bars of her cage

Yes, a house cat
A pretty little kitty easily fed and quickly tamed

I am a terrible liar

Legs aching to run
Teeth dying to chomp
She is not built to understand her own bindings

There is no other option now
She has become too feral, and I, too tired

Exhausted
from her pacing inside me
from her mad insistence

Her wild terrifies me

I must set her free
Domestication will destroy her with a painted smile

Once I loosed the lock
I prayed immediately for those in her wake

She streaked into darkness
Chains forgotten, cage swinging wide
My fear surged and abated as a bloodied tide

Her path was sure footed if wobbling
Ignoring even the juiciest tidbits for a definitive destination

Despite it all, she knew exactly where she was going

I watched her struggle to carry herself and felt
for the first time
true guilt overcome me

I broke her

This outrageous, stunning creature
Tore her apart as surely as skinning her alive
to hang her silent form from my wall

Silent is safer than untamed

I could see her powerful frame quaking
Starvation left her weak
I followed slowly behind
quiet
curiosity replacing fear in surprised increments

Her gigantic sighs of relief bellowed her rib cage
She stopped in an open field

Chest
open, closed
open, closed
Stripes of bone under skin

Thought she would collapse right there –
Feared it was too late –
I had murdered her in the slowest way
Year after year
a knife to the belly for every cry ignored

Instead, she looked up

Night sky clear and shining
her eyes transfixed on stars

She ate the light with her eyes

Labored breathing slowed
Puffs of cold breath easing in the dark

Her bony haunches settled into earth
and there she stayed

Tension eased from my bones
I sank into the ground to watch her
consuming the stars, the air, the night

I never knew it could be this way

God
she is beautiful

I will stay here with her
Follow when she leaves

Where she goes I will go

Ignore those who insist I starve her again
The condition of their acceptance is her submission

but they are rats
Tiny, squeaking, rabid with their own importance

The tiger ignores them
and so will I
Even in her depleted state, she would not poison her own
belly
They are beneath her

I will follow her
Trust her instincts

and maybe one day
she can forgive me for what I've done

Perhaps this is what surrender actually looks like
No muffled landing
but slow, concentrated undoing

A softening through scar tissue
Hardened skin smoothing its gristle
When shoulder blades relinquish their swords

Succumbing to what is-
the reality of accumulation
Piling
one heartbreak too many
Pushing
just one more bad decision
Pressing
another death, another loss

Between two road signs-
The You Before and *The You Beyond*
Surrender is laying in the crossroad dirt

Rain falling on your face
Dirt, cooling sludge beneath
As mud oozes through clenched fingers
Body heat wafting into setting sun

Surrendering right here
at the intersection
Letting that which weighed you down
stay in the dirt when you stand

It may be time for courageous grief
To deliver ashes from this burned flower bed
Give life to lamentation

It may be time to plant seeds
Harvesting bones from the wreckage
Sculpt and shape and sharpen
a new form from the old
Plunge them into a new patch of earth

It must be time
Anger is melting each molten step forward
Hair ripped away in hysterical mourning

Sow your salt
so no more dreaming can grow
Plant no roses in the past- it is bereft of water

The kalanchoe reminds me of the wild poppies
growing in my mother's front yard

She struggles to remember their name
I hold her hand, paper soft in the
sunlight,
and promise myself I will be
her memory every day

The mother of millions it's called,
        though Echidna
the mother of all monsters comes to mind

One populating the earth with seedlings,
the other with nightmares
Both repeating themselves over and over

I will plant a red kalanchoe on my porch
next to a potted gardenia in my
grandmother's yellow planter

For me
For the women in my life,
birthing themselves over and over and over

Butterflies in the Engine

There were monarchs caught in your air filter
and I secretly shuddered

The windshield of my Beetle
hosts thousands of sacrifices

and the God of Roads is grateful for both

It is a hungry Beast
Corpulent from my flesh and oil

It is gleeful in Its acceptance
of manic heartbreak hitting the pavement
to discover the healing only distance can provide

Tears fall relentlessly into
the maw of potholes
An elongated tongue emerges in the periphery
Mistaken for a traffic cone or mirage
It laps eagerly
Returns quickly

In my younger days,
I worshiped readily at Its mouth
Burning time and tires in effigy
Devout –
an Acolyte of Movement

The God of Roads was my lover
and I slicked along Its spine with windows down
My lust for freedom a tribute none could parallel

Yet,
there are monarchs
caught inside your engine,
broken and bright in the moving parts

I can feel the Beast rumble in delight
beneath my feet

Now, I question my religion

l had never considered the butterflies
nor the nature of a God who would
so greedily take what is best in our world
for Its own

<u>*A Mouse's Prayer*</u>

The world is too big today
No bigger than it normally is,
but its multitudes silence me nonetheless

I feel small

Small, grey, and incapable
of handling one more crumb

on this overladen table
before me

Shiver and shake apart
as the walls edge closer,
squeezing the banquet to splinters

I watch as the overripe oranges
hit the floor with a decidedly flourished squish

Not every day is like today
Just today is like today
And today I feel small

So, please
tell me I am gargantuan

Tell me I am a beast
Tell me that my breath is a howling ferocious wind

Tell me my mouth,
vividly lined with crunchers,
can snap this table and its contents in two
Swallow it whole
without a blink

Tell me I can do this,
this scrambling ahead,
this feeling my way in the darkness
An insistent pink nose surging forward in hope

The world and its adversities are fierce,
desperate and overwhelming
The planet,
claw-footed and deeply etched,
hunkers above,
and I am a mouse beneath

Tell me I'm a giant
so everything is not quite so impossible

I am pouring molasses on the past
Attempting to sweeten the gorges neglect formed
into something more palatable than the acid of this landscape

I could strangle on spit from hating you

Your voice
A dry, whiskey-smoke chuckle surrounds me
in the guise of men that conjure your silhouette in the heat
On the molasses road, an unshakable mirage

The sky splinters overhead in piercing, ragged rays
So bright it nauseates
Dust rising through broken desert gravel
You appear before me

In my most exposed moments
Teeth gritty with dirt and hair brittle from sun
In the deepest cusp of day, I understand

You are haunting me

Years have gone by but you linger
Fountains have filled, dried up, cracked and crumbled, yet
you remain

I could strangle myself for loving you

My heart is reckless
carving images of you into the stone of others
A disarming chuckle
A gap-toothed smile and sharpened hipbones
They are not themselves
They are you
Piss poor photocopies losing color after every repeat

Your ghost distorts the horizon ahead

Fear my future may never be empty of you
My feet will forever sink and stick to this ground
I will die here
Unable to move on
This sweet road will over take me and I will drown

Changing the Locks- an Exorcism

I will rip your shadow from my guts
if it is the last thing I do

Eviscerate myself to
unravel entrails foot by foot
Seeking out any pockets where you are hiding

Snaking through tendons to yank remaining tendrils lodged
inside
Splinters of you will find no shelter here

This is officially a non-hospitable environment

Move the spleen over
Check behind the kidneys
Toss out the appendix
Scrub your fingerprints from every inch of flesh

Combing through body until you are a distant memory
and I fasten myself shut

Pinning flesh together
A book binding, a chapter closing
Silver sewing needle and rainbow-colored thread marking my
belly
Anticipating the scar —
a reminder that today my life is mine

This is not your home
Not your story
You do not belong here
The ghost of you will no longer haunt me

Locks have been changed
and as often as you drive by –
you will gain no entrance

This is holy ground
This is sacred text
This is temple
This property has watchtowers and searchlights

I do not need your key back
You are un-invited
You are not welcome
This is my absolution

I will write you
Form you in ink
Mold your face through sentence
Mimic the cadence of your voice
Echo your words into prose

Each piece will be folded into paper castles
Crafted together with glue and patience
These castles will sit near the window

until they deflate and fall away
until they are just piles of paper
and not possibilities

I will write you
until I am empty

until I am free

I am swallowing gold today
because I am tired of hiding my gaps and cracks
Letting the warm, liquid ichor
fill in from the inside out

It will ooze to the surface, congealing
Harden into a second skin
Now you will see exactly where I am fused together

For years I stood lopsided and shrinking
clenching defiled thighs
Rounded shoulders holding weakened arms
at an awkward angle

I have stood this way
a splintered light bulb throwing shadows
vehemently claiming that I am fine

Don't look at me – I am fine
Don't worry about me – I am fine
Don't ask about me – I am fine
Please, please don't see me – I am fine

I have said this over and over
A rush to surety, as if all my storms are behind me
Covering the pile of dismantled pieces when others walk by
Too polite to contradict me
or too afraid
A manifestation of my own unfolding

Suffice to say
I don't have to think about being broken
as long as I appear put together

I have been shattered
I have been a puzzle, the pieces
a sum of everything that has tried to kill me
and failed

I swallow down gold
and lines appear across my body
Fastening skin to skin
Replenishing bone, filling muscle

Glossy tracks underneath my eyes
from weeping when one parent died, then the other

Glittering fingerprints on my forearms
where he would grab and shake me

Scars on my thighs from not one rape
but One, Two, Three and Four
One for each cardinal direction
One for each element
Spanning from five years old to five years ago

Reflective tic-tac-toe on my chest, over my heart
where I have loved and lost and loved and lost

My hope for the future
gleaming from all the places where I have put myself back
together
A walking night light, rivaling the stars above
Stronger, more complete than ever before

I am broken
and I am whole

Watering Wild No Flowers

No, I will not be quiet any more
No, you cannot lock me in
No
No
NO

Scuttling about my room
tracing the edges again and again
feels more familiar than the air creeping in

Trying not to make too much noise, though
I know how much you like your quiet

This room is stale
This room is empty

You removed all furniture and sharp objects
-including pens and paper
You never did like me writing about you

Can only stay quiet for so long
Only be nice so many times
Only scratch the yellow wallpaper so much until my hands
are raw

This is mayhem, living in bedlam
– but it is mine

Scraping bottom never felt so good
even if the walls are peeling goldenrod
Their cracking resounds in the silence

Can you hear it? I'm not certain you can
but I do

It is desperate water
engulfed into a parched and angry soul

This turmoil is mine
This cracking is mine
This No is mine...

No, until I believe it when I say it
No, until my No Muscle is hulked out
No, until you believe me when I say it
No, until it never occurs to me again that I cannot say No

I will scream No to the sky in undulation
until it breaks the ceiling
and No rains down, soaking my clothes and wetting the floor

Bursting this room open, bringing in sunshine, turning this
shamble into a garden

It was dangerous of you to put me in here
Stupid of you to silence me

I am now larger and more articulate than I have ever been

I will walk on my muddy fields of Wild Nos
and bundle them in my arms
– smelling their sweet, honeysuckle pollen
Face and hands coated in No Dust

I will paper my body with No
I will fill my vases with saffron No Flowers
No Vines will crawl through wreckage, crumbling the stones

This room cannot hold my riotous Nos

This room will not hold me
        and you are right to be afraid

My mother gave me a patch of earth for snapdragons
Her concession to mud-crawling wildness
My acquiescence to accepting affection

The Lady and the Trampolining Monkey/Child
Lipstick stealing, tree climbing, pantyhose ripping,
whirlwind

Her remote beauty gleamed from
afar like the nail polish on her
fingertips
I knew I was *other*
compared to such gentility

And she, more exasperated than accessible,
helped me cultivate the wild flowers of my choosing

When both of us, elbow deep in dirt,
could recognize
the smudges on the other's face, the tempered brows
over serious selections of seedlings, bridges built
themselves over the rivers running between us

Though that square of dirt now stands
quiet a very stubborn snapdragon or two
will burst through each spring-

and she still says, eyes shining *Those are my daughter's flowers*

The High Places of a Feline Heart

My heart sometimes retreats to high places
Tops of mountains with blue daisies
Rooftop bars with glasses of sweet red
States with high elevation
Cities with skyscrapers

I would love to think it's a poetic musing,
gaining perspective on lofty aspirations
A shrewd, meditative escape to (literal) higher principles

Really though,
times like this resemble my fat, orange tabby
more than anything else
Huffy, poofy, cranky,
and climbing to the top of the Cat Tower
to survey the treacherous landscape with cynical,
vertical slits

It is from this vantage,
critical of the hoi polloi,
wondering why the inhabitants of life
insist on being so *common* and terribly vulgar,
that my heart bathes luxuriously in the silence

Naps are plentiful,
hearing is selective-
even when promised extra pets, yummy snacks,
and a pile of hair ties
Save your bribes, dear friends!

My heart, when it retreats,
finds its castle and stays put
(Until it's *certain* the world is free, albeit temporarily,
of vacuums, dogs, and vexatious spirits)

So, if you stumble on my heart
at the top of the crest, glass of wine in hand,
whiskers twitching slightly in the evening breeze,
best leave it in peace
I'm not ready to come down just yet, thank you very much

I have pushpins in the bottom of my heart,
fallen into the crevices from pictures I've put up and taken
down
I'm pretty sure they're tangled with those missing shoelaces
You see how silly it is to love me from the bottom of your
heart?
No one wants to drink the last dregs of coffee
I don't know what's down there in your depths
I could love you from my left ventricle, or if I ever find that
paint covered
step-stool, love you from my aorta

It's pretty cluttered in here
Need time to clear out the cobwebs and organize the junk,
scampering with critters and covered in dust
Towards the bottom I've got my hands full with socks that
have no mate,
and secrets that are trying to weasel their way up through the
tricuspid
No one ever warned me how tenacious secrets can be-
if I knew, I wouldn't have kept so many

So if you insist on loving me,
find it in the ends of your toes or from the lengths of your
hair,
pull this love from tingly fingertips,
find this love in unoccupied spaces
where you are unencumbered
and I will do the same

When the soft animal of me
hungers, desires, and thirsts I
heed her call with a war whoop

A towering, storm-ridden tiger
roar reverberating against rocks
Against the stars themselves

So gargantuan that no one can mistake the din-
the primordial scream of a woman answering
herself

Yes! I say

Yes to your hunger

I will feed you mouths and hearts and tongues

I will fill your belly with boundaries

and affirmations

I will nourish and sedate you

You are right to be hungry

and I will answer you

So, she is fed

Yes! I say
Yes to your desire
I will send silk and flesh and
bone beneath your hands, your
teeth
Give you the world to suck dry and fuck up
Grant you consenting bodies that need you in
return
You are right to desire
and I will answer you

So, she is contented

Yes! I say, finally
Yes to your thirst
Yes a thousand times to the
nectar you crave
To water and wine, and liquid
cool words sliding down your
throat
You are right to thirst
and I will answer you

So, she is satiated

Even if she does not respond at first
Even if a life of bruising deprivation has left her
starved and battered and unnerved
Even if she has never allowed herself
to thirst, to want, to hunger, to need with a tornado of
desperation

I do not fear her storm

Yet each time I answer her cries a
bruise is lifted from soft flesh
Each time she is fed and fucked and
heard
a violation is replaced with dignity

Each time I say Yes to her-
Yes to the beast of her
Yes to the storm of her
Yes to the power that electrifies and consumes
those that fear her

She and I become closer to one

The Gatekeeper Wears Acrylics

There's a dragon-lady at the Gates to my heart
I hired her on a slow Friday night
when it started to become just a
Little. Too. Much.
She patted my cheek with her papery hand
and said, "You're such a treasure, chicky"

It's not that I can't work without her,
but recently things have cut too deep
One too many usurpers slipped past the skin,
found a well-lit pathway of insecurity,
sailing down the heart strings to hunker down for a beer
and raucous laughter in the depths of my being

It takes forever to disentangle the little shits from the muscles
and sinew
(It's internal, things get sticky and clingy in here)
My energy is better spent on something else wonderful like
dancinglovingdreamingfuckingsleepingeatingdrawingpoetrybe
lieving
than yanking unmentionables from my breast

So when I say "dragon-lady"
it isn't just her spit-fire attitude and dry skin
Literally, she's part dragon,
with her scaling azure blue tail
curling cat-like around the security booth at the Gate
Rocking acrylics so long she can barely text
on her poppy pink cell phone
(Although, the clove cigarettes she insists
on smoking have greened the tips a bit)

Hired on the spot,
guaranteed overtime with full benefits,
One look at her and invaders scrambled for the exit
without a by-your-leave
She chuckles dryly when that happens,
a sound like autumn leaves crunching under well-calloused
toes
in unusual orchestration
Same color autumn as her perfectly coiffed, helmet-secure
hair
Admitted to rollers and silk every night, just to
"Solidify the grace of an experienced dragon, sugar muffin"

She cackles like leaves again

Perfect for the job, really
Especially now that
I. Am. Done.
with letting just anyone or anything in
Done with leaving thoughtless, selfish, disorganized, loud
aggressors in my heart
and unwelcome ghosts
(The dragon-lady is a Certified Exorcist, as well
It was at the bottom of her online resume, near her
cosmetology license)
No more traipsing around my insides, no ma'am,
not with the dragon-lady at the Gate
And not just humans, either
Ideas, thoughts, music, concepts, beliefs, obligations, work,
art, all have to pass inspection

Rocking a "No, but thanks for stopping by, dearie" like it's
going out of style,
she filters and sorts, denies, unceremoniously ejects, and
incinerates
anyone or anything
who insists they have a right to enter
(Truth be told, she'll kick some back up to the Brain for good
measure,
but mostly she trusts her own immediate judgement)

"It's a sacred space, sweet cakes" she intones one day,
clove smoke encircling the actual smoke emitting from her
engorged nostrils
"Be careful what you let in"

It'll take some time to completely trust her instincts,
her take-no-prisoners, no-fucks-to-give attitude
I spent most of my life being a revolving door with no
discernment
But, no longer

We'll adjust to each other
Soon I'll learn to not wince as she sends someone else
packing
with a singed backside and distinct smell of cloves
Things are cleaner, quieter, and more joyful around here
When something is let through the Gates,
it wholeheartedly belongs here

with my chest lighter for their invitation

The Gatekeeper is part dragon after all,
and protecting her gold is what she does best

I wish you were here
so I could read this to you

But then again
not sure how I feel about you being inside me this way
Maybe you should buy me dinner first?

But I don't like people watching me eat, either
Just reminds me of
when lettuce was lunch and television was dinner
and exercising six hours every day went unremarked except
for-
"We're so proud of your dedication"

Today
puberty is still quaking beneath my kneecaps
like I stashed it there for a rainy fucking day and it's monsoon
season in the desert
I feel 60 pounds heavier
and smaller than I've ever been
13 years old
with overalls and craft glitter stuck to my face

Craft. Glitter.
Not tiny little tubs of makeup "shimmer"
Gigantic globs of craft glitter glue
in my desperate efforts to be an effortlessly pretty girl
You know the ones
Tiny enough to be approachable
Quiet enough to not to be a threat
Terrific at acquiescence
The kind of cute that was mold-able and fuck-able and leave-
able

I was a piece of construction paper
amidst instructional pamphlets of femininity
Cutting myself into stars and skinny arms and lopsided hearts
and hourglass figures and rainbows
with shimmering outlines

I am her today
Lopsided and a just little bit shiny
trying way too hard and hoping it will be endearing in its
sincerity

I am wishing you were here and so grateful you are not
and not entirely sure of what I'm trying to say
except-

I don't know how to stay away from you
Some mornings, you are my first thought before anything else
and when I think about adventures, random car rides,
and selfies,
you are in every picture
That I've never been afraid to eat in front of you
In fact, I order the hot chocolate with the extra
marshmallows every time

You call forth the me that
is still awkward, still Bedazzling her backpack and still
counting Magic the Gathering cards
and
you don't lay her to rest
so much as love her so fiercely I wonder
what was wrong with her in the first place

My pixie cut is
one part magic
one part fuck-you-up

Deconstruction
Confronting my face every day
with no room for flounce

A gauntlet
with no place for your parade
A mirror
where cracked masculinity crumbles

Ground zero
to recharge batteries of bodily autonomy
I come here post-death
Post-heartbreak
Post-rape

There is no cut sharper than
"You'd be so much prettier with longer hair!"
As if pretty was the point
As if beautiful was a place to live and pay taxes to
As if attracting you is the end of my every journey-
barefoot, alive, feral

No concern of mine
your sexuality shrinks
with the length of my locks

I was not made to be consumed

My pixie cut is my hiding place
My tree house
I'm hanging upside-down
Stripping off my mama's pantyhose after a night at the ballet

Hoarding red lipstick
Painting my face with war symbols, practicing my aim

My pixie cut is
when my hair is not a handle to grab and bow my back

My solace

A homecoming

and just before you decide
you understand my resurrections –
I will grow my hair
snake it around your neck
and hang you with your own expectations

My anxiety is a fluffy, little bunny

She blends into the environment,
hiding in the half-light of sunrise and sunset
You would never know she's there

Until, BAM!
Sensing danger before I do,
she gets us the hell out of there!
(Or tries to)
Taking off across the earth,
feet moving only a shade faster than her fierce, tiny heart

If caught,
or even imagining a trap ahead,
she'll scream, shrill and blood-curdling

Puts the Xena kick into rabbit-kicking,
tufts of luxurious fur flying every which way
until the predator is defeated,
or we're far enough away to breathe again

It is only because I was taught not to trust her,
only because bunnies are not supposed to know better
than the mighty development of the prefrontal cortex,

that I have fought her so hard, for so very long,
to both our detriment
this warrior-rabbit wasn't exactly wrong

Despite her strength and tenacity,
and hell-bent insistence that she is saving us,
(Truly, she should be an enormous, Paleolithic, scale-covered hare)
she will not get to make the call every time,

but neither will she reside in the periphery

When we sat close enough to touch
I would twirl the golden watch around her wrist
Feel the smooth grooves slide beneath my sticky fingers
Ritualistic and soothing

Spin the watch three times
A binding spell to keep her near

She wore the gold band unconsciously
For every outfit
In every photo

She lamented the loss of diamonds, the family crest, before I
was born
What are these things to me?
Cold and sparkling idioms from a distant past

Those were not my treasures

Spin the watch three times again

Her smile was the winter sun
I wanted nothing more than to be enveloped by her warmth
Though she tried and tried
nothing could bridge the distance of seasons

I would hug her tightly to me and say- *I'm not finished yet*
when she pulled away

Just spin the watch three more times

On my own wrist
I wear it now though it's broken
Feeling the smoothed grooves and softened edges

In the end
when I hugged her goodbye, she pulled me close, tighter
and said –
I'm not finished yet

It was a summer sun heating my face just before the night fell

To breathe and swell
with incoming wind
is the only option left

You cannot fight the air
Gales make mortals of even Hercules

We are aspens in the woods
with aspirations of being uprooted from one another

We stand golden leaves alight looking upon one
another with smug independence even as our
systems grow together beneath

We are
one being
There is no pulling apart what is

Our roots share secrets
while we sleep above
content with the delusion that we dream alone

Our white limbs twining
together boughs and elbows
bumping when our attention is
elsewhere

But when the wind blusters

I lean into you and we tangle even more

Identity amidst the multitudes is

what we seek

even if our most holy solace is found in one another in
the end

I cannot carry a stone.
They don't tell you this in the stories. With a mind like a stone, I cannot take you anywhere, which is equal parts depressing and relieving.

The twists and turns of the mindscape suck a person under, body and soul.

One minute, you (The you beyond all the assumptions, lace, and trappings.) are the observer of the mindscape. The sky blue slate over which thought clouds dance. Fluffy and seemingly insignificant, these cottontails float along, and in their step, intoxication begins.

You relinquish that gentle hold on the present and follow me down the rabbit hole.

Perhaps you awaken quickly and remove yourself once more to the quiet blue expanse.
Or, you don't awaken, spinning on and on, winging from one thought to the next, until you are exhausted and crave any respite over all else. You fall upon the nearest soft landing. You can waste days, years, lifetimes, following the clouds.

But I, I cannot carry stones.

And if you, perchance, were to make yourself a stone, leaving the clouds to their luscious meanderings, while taking hold of none, then I, dear reader, could take you nowhere.

1

I crave roses made of sunbeams and blood
to stuff in my pockets and leave a path as they fall from the
hole
in my jeans
Just in case I get lost
Yellow-red petals will trail into sunset,
bleeding into the next sunrise

2

Genuardi's refrigerated cases full of golden, yellow roses with
crimson under-petals, greeted me with frigid blast and the
wonder of new experience. There are no Genuardi's where I
live. There are no stone houses with turrets and candy-
colored trimming. There are no grids here, but wandering,
curving streets, full of low-hanging lights and U-turns. I have
never been here before.

3

I might be northeast of the last ray of sun when my traveling
is done,
with empty pockets and heart pumping full
It will be a conclusion of dreams-
Stranger things have happened, where I've never been before

4

I had no money for the roses but tomorrow is another day.

5

You will wonder where I have gone
Follow the trail
Follow me

I am bluebird
with breast beating
Azure-footed veins
cascade behind divinely lofted wings

I am wind
to carry this weight,
padlocks dropping,
clinking below as new heights surround me

I am air whistling
a full-throated song
a freedom song
a benediction
a lamentation

I will not excuse myself
or my opal eyes

There are bluebirds in this blood,
beneath this skin

There is wind to lift and songs to be sung

I am the benediction
with sky awaiting my flight

Wishes Like Snow

I gathered wishes from deserted roadside when you left me
Bundled with scattering of violet wildflowers

Stuck to fingers
Clung to lips
Tenacious in their need

A crumpled hand
A puff of air
Breathed into being on dry seeded snow

Cascaded into oncoming wind, lifted away

Set free to enact themselves upon the world
and return gently
– a kiss of fallow winter on the brows
of their redeemers

Like so many things

A breath of life
A release
A return home

Court Winterborne is a native Texan, transplanted to North Carolina via New Mexico, Wales, Chicago and New York.

She was the editor for the *Gravity Hill Vol. 3* literary magazine at St. Andrew's University Press, which also published her first book of poetry *Season For Season*. She published her second book of poetry *Wild Horses*, as well as edited the first two editions of *Light as a Feather: An Anthology of Resilience,* through Swimming with Elephants Press. She has contributed short fiction to **Corbeau Media** and **Main Street Rag**, along with articles about feminism and the #metoo movement for *Psychology Today*.

Court is a hair/wig, makeup and special effects designer for film, Broadway and opera. She resides in North Carolina with her partner and two spoiled kitty cats.

www.ingramcontent.com/pod-product-compliance
Lightning Source LLC
Chambersburg PA
CBHW071511130726
47997CB00006B/2489